Tutor 2 Tutor:
A Guide to Earning Wealth Through Tutoring

LaTishia L. Jordan

Whitney King

ISBN: 1507737327
ISBN-13:9781507737323

DEDICATION

LaTishia Jordan - This book is dedicated to my mother, Pamela M. Thomas, for her kindness and devotion, and for her endless support in all of my endeavors; her selflessness will always be remembered.

Whitney King: All of the late nights are for my two beautiful children. All of the knowledge shared is for every person desiring to operate a tutoring business in order to help a child reach their maximum potential.

CONTENTS

Acknowledgments   v

Determine Your Niche   6

Ask Yourself the 5 W's   7

Determining Your Pricing   10

Writing Your Business Plan   15

Policies   22

Materials   25

Marketing   26

Consultation   28

Session Notes   30

ACKNOWLEDGMENTS

We hereby acknowledge the following people and organizations for their contributions to this book:
B.O.B. Group
Dr. Will Moreland

Determine Your Niche

When starting out in business, it is important to find an attractive niche that will help you establish your business. When you create a niche, it keeps your business from struggling with more established tutoring companies and will allow your profit margin to be big early on. Higher profit margins are essential for the expansion of your tutoring business. So what is a niche?

Entreprnuer.com defines niche as "A portion of a market that you've identified as having some special characteristic and that's worth marketing to." In shortest terms, it's something that sets your business apart from others. Your niche will be based on who is your target audience. Is it your goal to serve those that are underprivileged and cannot afford to pay for tutoring elsewhere or are you interested in high paying clientele? Are you working with kids or adults? Are you serving general education students or students with special needs? Because you are competing with bigger and more established tutoring companies, you have to be able to offer something that will make families decide to go with your services. There are several things that you could offer as your niche:

- Weekly lesson plans
- Virtual Lessons
- Support at Parent/Teacher Meetings
- Detailed Reports after each lesson

The most important thing about selecting your niche is that the demand exceeds supply. When this happens, you are able to charge a higher rate therefore increasing your profit margin. Entreprenuer.com states that a niche has 5 good qualities:

- It takes you where you want to go--in other words, it conforms to your long-term vision.
- Somebody else wants it--namely, customers.
- It's carefully planned.
- It's one-of-a-kind, the "only game in town."
- It evolves, allowing you to develop different profit centers and still retain the core business, thus ensuring long-term success.

Remember, being in a particular field isn't the same thing as having a niche. For example, a company could be in the restaurant industry, but their niche is that you park to order your food and then someone brings it to you. The goal isn't to serve everybody, but to be the best at who you can serve. Pick what your strengths are, study those strengths constantly to make them better, and sell those.

Exercise:
What is your niche?

_____

_____

_____

_____

_____

_____

_____

_____

Ask Yourself the 5 W's

The main points discussed in this reading all tie together. The previous section was about finding your niche. This continues into the 5 W's of starting a new business. A majority of entrepreneurs start businesses based on some type of knowledge about a particular industry. This knowledge is usually from prior experience. After deciding to become an entrepreneur, this person then takes on a new role [business owner] and the person isn't skilled in this area. This could lead to a host of problems later. The objective of the 5W's is to help new and rising entrepreneurs avoid common and costly mistakes.

- **Why** - Why do you make doing this task a priority in your day? What is the purpose of your business? Can your clients verbalize your purpose? If you can't answer these questions easily, you may need to arrange to go deeper with the coaches that created this book. Everyone involved in your business {business partners, family, clients, etc.} should cohesively agree on your purpose. If this isn't the case, your business will fall apart.

- **Where** - Where is your market? Is your market geographically based or is it a certain group of people. Regardless of what your market is, you should have a clear understanding of what it is and who the ideal customer is. Exercise: create a collage of your target customer. This should include where you can find them, what they may watch, drink, eat, etc.) This will eventually help you with marketing to your potential clients.

- **What** - Now that you know who you want as a customer, what are you asking them to purchase from you? What problem are you going to solve for this client? What makes your solution to their problem better or different from someone else in the marketplace? You should also take the time to create a SWOT analysis (Strengths, weaknesses, opportunities, and threats). Can you adapt your solutions to meet the changing needs of the client? You want your clients to be able to describe to another potential client the benefits of your services. It's important that you know the answers to these questions; if not your sales and marketing plans won't work.

- **Who** - This is, in our opinion, the most critical question of the 5W's. Who is on your team? Who is going to live the mission, vision, and purpose that you've set in order to lead the business to victory? Keep people on your team because they are valuable to your mission, not because they are close friends and family. Are you willing to receive/provide trainings that will make your team stronger?

- **When** - You must keep the future, the end goal in mind at all times. How far do you want to take this? Will you just be operating this business temporarily? Are you only doing this to make a few extra dollars during the year or are you trying to establish something more lucrative? Will this grow or will you sell it. Be sure to map out your plans regardless of how you want it to end.

The information presented above can be applied to opening to just about any business. The tutoring industry is HUGE so it is vital that you have clarity on why you are in it. Although I love the beach, I wouldn't dare go and become a lifeguard.

Exercise:
Who do you want to service?

_____

_____

_____

_____

Why do you want to tutor?

_____

_____

_____

_____

What do you want to tutor?

_____

_____

_____

_____

When do you want to tutor?

_____

_____

_____

_____

Exercise:
Where do you want to tutor?

_____

_____

_____

_____

_____

Determining Your Pricing

Raise your hand if you like your day job. Now raise your hand if you would still go if you got paid less that what you get right now. Now it's obvious that you would still tutor regardless of pay because you are taking the time to invest in your business, BUT it takes a lot of time and effort into preparing lessons, connecting with families, marketing, and then finally tutoring. It won't feel as rewarding to you if you don't compensate yourself appropriately. This will in turn affect the way your client feels about you because it will no doubt put a strain on your performance. As we know, word of mouth is one of the biggest marketing tools in this industry, so the family will of course spread the nasty message about your service.

Save yourself the time and headache and just charge what you feel you are worth from the beginning. Everyone will not like your fee and you should be comfortable in knowing what you are worth so that you do not have to hassle and negotiate. Thinking back to when I first started tutoring, I remember making my prices so low thinking that would bring me a load of clients. I had 1 and I only had 1 for months. I had prospects, but no one would register. I met another teacher that advised me to look at what other tutors were charging in the area. I was as least $20 under. I was astonished. It was then determined that people perceived me as inexperienced because I was charging so much less. I raised my price so that it was only $5 less. I was less than everyone else, but my price was now deemed competition.

You should take into account what others in the area are charging. It is imperative. You don't want to undercharge or overcharge. Many tutors fail because they think they need to come in lower than others in order to gain clients. Answer this, would you purchase a BMW for $700. It would make you think something must be wrong with it. This is the same way clients think about tutors. If it is too low, they must be a beginner, not experienced, and desperately needing cash. When you know your value and stick with it, your clients will respect your value also. Pricing is also based off of what you will be providing to your clients. Will you be providing supplies or will they be responsible for them? Are you creating lesson plans or are you only working on homework?

Exercise:
Will you provide supplies?

_____

_____

_____

_____

_____

Are you creating lesson plans or working on homework?

_____

_____

_____

_____

What is your competition charging?

_____

_____

_____

_____

_____

_____

- **Invoicing your customers** - Sending invoices is another way to put your business on the market as something serious. Now it is your choice how you decide to bill your customers. This can be day to day, weekly, and bi-weekly or however you and the client decide. This can also vary depending on what works best with you and your client. Billing is a way to keep track of what money you have coming into the business so that you can plan and budget your business expenses. See the sample invoice on the next page.

INVOICE

Your Company Slogan

Date: [Click to select date]
INVOICE # [100]

To

[Name]
[Company Name]
[Street Address]
[City, ST ZIP Code]
[Phone]
Customer ID [ABC12345]

Salesperson	Job	Payment Terms	Due Date
		Due on receipt	

Qty	Description	Unit Price	Line Total
		Subtotal	
		Sales Tax	
		Total	

Make all checks payable to [Your Company Name]

Thank you for your business!

[Your Company Name] [Street Address], [City, ST ZIP Code] Phone [phone] Fax [fax] [email]

- **Receiving Payments** - How will you accept payments? One of the biggest tools out right now is PayPal. Another is square. This makes your business more legit than just saying cash only. Also, having receipts looks legit as well. Will you accept checks? What is your policy on late payments? Do you have a refund policy? All of these are important questions to have answers to before taking your first client. How often will you charge clients; per session, weekly, bi-weekly, monthly, etc. Have this established and stick to it. Now of course in the business world, there are exceptions that can be made in the name of customer satisfaction. Just remember don't let a few instances of customer satisfaction become a customer habit.

Exercise:
How will you accept payments?

_____

_____

_____

Will you accept checks?

_____

_____

_____

What is your policy on late payments?

_____

_____

_____

Do you have a refund policy?

_____

_____

_____

- **Registering your business** - I remember when I first registered my business. It was a very proud moment for me. This let my family, friends, and even clients know that everything I did was professional. This is something that will put you in the game as being taken serious. You can go about this two ways. You can manage your funds and just add them onto your taxes. Taking this route would consider you a sole proprietor. If you decide to come up with a business name, you could register as an LLC, non-profit, and a few other options. You should certainly discuss the options with a tax representative, a lawyer, and you can even look into more resources with the Small Business Administration.

Writing a Business Plan

In this section we want to answer several questions for you about the business plan, why you need a business plan, what to include in the business plan, and how to format the business plan.

What is a business plan?
A business plan is a road map that outlines your business, pinpoints your goals, how you plan to achieve those goals and serves as a guide for your business.

Why do you need a business plan?
Let's just step outside of this book for a moment and say that you were on a trip to a place you have never been before. How would you know how to get there? You would do one of a few things: ask for directions, read a map, or use a GPS system.

Think of your business plan as the same thing, a map, or GPS system for your business. Reasons for creating a business plan include:
- defining your business
- provide information necessary for outside funding
- to monitor the progression of the business
- so that you know how to market the business
- it allows you a chance to map out the direction of your business

…….and those are just a few of the many reasons you should have a business plan.

What do you include in your business plan?
All good business plans should include the following:
- **A Cover Page** – This seems like a no brainer but you won't believe how many people forget to include a cover page with their contact information leaving a

potentially great business plan on the table because the investor does not have a method of contacting the business owner.

Exercise:
What contact information should go on your Business Plan?

_____

_____

_____

_____

_____

- **An Executive Summary** – This is like an elevator pitch, this is where you will put the most important facts about your business. You want to introduce your business, introduce the products or services that you offer, and most importantly it should tell the reader why they should invest in your business whether that be through time or money. Keep in mind that it is probably the only portion of your business plan that most people will actually read.

Exercise:
What is your elevator pitch?

_____

_____

_____

_____

_____

- **A Company Summary** – This section of the business plan looks at how all of the different components of your business fit together, including information about the environment of your business and the success factors that you feel will make your business successful and profitable. It should include a succinct opening paragraph about your company, the ownership of the company and what type of business entity it is, startup summary which would include startup costs and assets as well as the company location.

Exercise:
Give a description of your business?

_____

_____

_____

What type of business entity does your business have? (i.e. Sole Proprietor, LLC, etc.)

_____

_____

What are your startup costs?

_____

_____

_____

What are your assets?

_____

_____

_____

Where is the company located? If you don't have a brick and mortar facility what address will you use?

_____

_____

- **Services or Products** – In this section you want to discuss what you are offering. Most tutors only have their services to discuss in this section but remember they must be broken down by types of services for example if you plan to offer tutoring and test prep then each one of these will be a different service or product that you offer.

Exercise:
What products or services will you offer?

_____

_____

_____

_____

_____

- **A Strategic Analysis** – Also known as a SWOT analysis this is an acronym for the four major components of the analysis: Strengths, Weaknesses, Opportunities, and Threats. The SWOT Analysis forces you to think about your business in a whole new way. Your strengths and weaknesses are internal so they can be changed but it may take some time and your opportunities and threats and external so they are happening in the market and you cannot really stop them from occurring. Creating a SWOT analysis from the beginning will help you to avoid headaches in the long run. See the template for a SWOT Analysis on the next page.

SWOT Analysis

Strengths	Weaknesses
Opportunities	**Threats**

- **Marketing Plan** – The marketing plan is a plan that outlines the company's marketing plan for the period covered by the plan. This plan shows what steps to take in order to accomplish the businesses marking objectives. Your marketing plan will include the following:
  - o A description of your competitors
  - o A marketing budget
  - o A pricing strategy
  - o The demand for the product or service that you are offering

Exercise:
Who are your competitors?

_____

_____

_____

_____

What is your marketing budget?

_____

_____

_____

What is your pricing strategy?

_____

_____

_____

What is the demand for the products and/or services that you are offering?

_____

_____

_____

_____

- **Personnel Plan** – This portion of the business plan gives you the opportunity to discuss the following:
    - o Types of employees you will need (i.e. tutors)
    - o Employee job descriptions
    - o Employee knowledge and skills requirements
    - o Employee pay

Exercise:
What types of employees do you need?

_____

_____

_____

_____

What are the job descriptions for each position you will hire for?

_____

_____

_____

_____

_____

What knowledge, skills, and abilities should your employees possess?

_____

_____

_____

_____

_____

Exercise:
How much will you pay your employees?

_____

_____

_____

_____

- **Financial Plan** – This is the final and probably most difficult portion of your business plan not because of the content but because most of us just don't like to discuss finances.

Policies

In order to avoid unnecessary conflict within your business you want to make sure you have policies and procedures established for your company. In this section we will go over policies and procedures that you will need for your company and provide you with templates to assist you in establishing your own. Some of the policies you want to have established are listed below:

- Attendance – This policy tells the client/parent what your expectations are as far as attending tutoring sessions. Make sure you spell out EXACTLY what you would like for them to know because your signed policies become a legal contract between the two parties.

- Hourly Rate – Determine what you will charge hourly and then how you want to receive those payments.

- Payment – This policy provides the responsible party with information on how you would like to be paid and when you would like to be paid. Some tutors want to only be paid by check or debit card, some want to be paid monthly and some prefer weekly payments or payments by session. Whatever it is that you decide to do spell that out early and make sure to review it with the responsible party during your initial consultation.

Exercise:

What is your attendance policy?

_____

_____

_____

_____

What is your hourly rate?

_____

_____

_____

_____

_____

_____

What will your payment policy entail?

_____

_____

_____

_____

_____

- Invoicing and Payments – It is best that you provide the client/parent with an invoice so they are aware of what they owe you and what they are paying for. Your invoice should include your contact information, the responsible parties contact information, account information for the responsible party , what services you rendered, the costs of those services, and how much they owe you.

- Late Payments – This policy will cover you if a parent pays late especially if they are habitual about making late payments. Make sure that you have established due dates/days for your clients and have a monetary value in place that they must pay if they are late with a payment.

- Cancellations – We know that at times there is a need to cancel a session without notice but sometimes parents will get "too busy" and just forget about the session so you want to make sure you have a cancellation policy that covers you when times like these arise. We recommend having a 24 hour cancellation policy meaning you are to receive notice 24 hours in advance if someone plans to cancel a session. With that cancelled session (which should be paid if it is not 24 hours advanced notice or if you have a monthly payment plan in place) the student should be provided with an opportunity to make up the session in the same week. If they fail to do so they have paid for the session and will not be reimbursed for it.

Exercise:
What is your cancellation policy?

_____

_____

_____

_____

_____

_____

- Make-up Sessions – Make-up sessions are allowed for those times when the client becomes ill, or has an emergency of some sort and has to cancel the session. Make sure you put in writing times when make-up sessions are allowed and the procedures one must follow in order to schedule a make-up session.

Exercise:
What is your make-up policy?

_____

_____

_____

_____

_____

_____

- Refunds – You will run into situations in which a parent/client will request a refund. If you have the refund policy spelled out then they will know when this is possible and when it is not.

Exercise:
What is your refund policy?

_____

_____

_____

_____

_____

_____

Materials

Deciding on what materials to use in a tutoring session is probably one of the hardest things there is to do when establishing your tutoring business. This is a difficult tasks because they are so many types of materials out there and you will find that some will work for some students that may not work with others. Our recommendation is to get your hands on a set of textbooks being used by the school district in which you services and determine a set of websites that you can use as a resource for additional materials. Once your business starts to grow you can decide whether or not you would like to invest in additional materials or begin to create your own.

Marketing

Once you have decided on who you will service and the geographic region that you will service you can start planning tactics that you will use to market your business. There are several ways to market your tutoring business so in this section we will cover the ones that we feel will produce the most clients. We do recommend that you utilize as many free options as possible before paying for marketing and advertising.

Start with the schools <u>Guidance Office</u> now if you live in a larger district try to only take on 5-10 schools and once you have conquered those schools you will find that your work speaks for itself and other schools will start to come to you for services. Speak with the guidance counselor and introduce yourself, business, and the services that you offer. Ask if there is a place in which you can leave materials for parents or students such as brochures, fliers, or a poster that advertises your services.

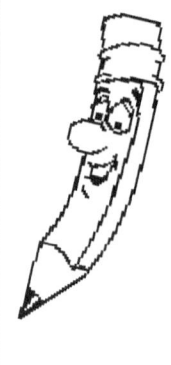

Exercise:
List five schools that you would like to contact and partner up with.

_____

_____

_____

_____

_____

_____

<u>Pediatric doctors and dentists offices</u> are also a great place to leave materials. You can handle this one of two ways: either ask the office manager if you can just leave the materials in the waiting area of you can see if there is a way to partner with the office and receive recommendations from them for potential clients in turn you can recommend these offices to your students as well.

<u>Grocery Stores/ Coffee Shops</u> are also great places to advertise your services because most have a community service bulletin board in which you can post information about your business.

Exercise:
List at least five pediatric offices, grocery stores, and coffee shops that you can advertise with.

_____

_____

_____

_____

_____

<u>Community Centers</u> are also a great place to advertise for free. They also have bulletin boards in which you can place information about your business and the services that you offer. Not only do they attract kids they also attract a lot of parents as this is a place in which parents and their children like to hang out and enjoy recreational activities. More than likely you will have to obtain permission from the office prior to posting any information on your business so make sure you ask first.

<u>Public Libraries</u> are also a good place to advertise as you get a lot of parents and students who come through daily. Just like the community centers make sure you have permission to posts the information prior to doing so. You will pick up a lot of home school clients in community centers and libraries.

Exercise:
List five libraries and/or community centers that you can contact that may be interested in advertising your tutoring business.

_____

_____

_____

_____

The BEST form of advertising for a tutoring business has to be <u>WORD OF MOUTH</u>. Word of Mouth is the easiest way to advertise your business because all it requires is a conversation with everyone that you know who may be able to refer clients to you. Make sure everyone is aware that you have a new business and what services you offer and ask them to help you spread the word to everyone that they know. Once you get started and have clients you can also ask those clients for referrals. If you know of any teachers add them to your network of marketers because they can also refer students to you.

Exercise:
List five people who you can contact and introduce to your business.

_____

_____

_____

_____

_____

Consultation

One of the most important aspects of the sale is the initial consultation. The consultation says the most about your business and the way that you operate the business. The first thing that you want to do introduce yourself followed by finding out the name of the parent and the child in which they are seeking tutoring for. As soon as you gather that information from the parent reference them by their last name but reference the child by their first name.

It is key to remember you are not cold-calling as the parent has taken out the time to seek you and your services out. Provide them with information on you and your business and how you plan to assist their child but don't sound like you are reading a sales script.

After the introductions allow the parent to do the majority of the talking. However if the parent is hesitant have a list of questions you can use to probe them and make them elaborate on their child and the child's needs. Make sure you ask questions that will give you information on previous strategies and the results from trying them. You may even find it helpful to talk to the child and see what information you can gather from them.

Discuss what your plans are for the child and how the next session will go. Go over any paperwork that you need signed with the parent and get all policies signed at that time this includes discussing your payment policies as well and make sure that you all have exchanged contact information.

Once you have all of the information that you need it will be time to decide on a schedule and set a time and location for your initial session. Leave time at the end of the conversation to answer any questions, comments, or concerns of the parent or the child.

Sessions

Remember that first impressions are lasting impressions so while in your first tutoring session always keep that in mind. Most students come to tutoring with a lot of pre-conceived notions. It is important to treat all students with respect, listen to them, and help them in discussing their need.

If you are having the session in a public place like the library make sure you have a method of the tutee knowing that is you. Display a sign so that the tutees will be able to see and identify you and acknowledge them with a smile and a friendly greeting.

Depending on what type of program you have established you can handle the session a few ways and they are listed below:

- Homework Support: In this type of session you have been hired to assist the student with homework so you should ask that they take their homework out and then ask what they are having difficulty with and work through the homework problems with them.
- Curriculum Program: In this program you will have a curriculum designed by the staff with the aid of an assessment test for that particular student.

Set and articulate small reasonable goals and end the session.

Take notes and write comments on what you worked on and the results of the session. You can choose how often to send session notes to parents as some parents will not want the notes they will just want to see the improvements in grades however, keep a copy on file so that if the parent asks you will have it.

Exercise:
What type of session will you offer?

_____

_____

_____

_____

_____

_____

Session Notes

Name of Client: _____

Length of Session: _____

Subject: _____

Energy: _____

Preparation: _____

Progress: _____

Teacher: _____

Date: _____

Tutor: _____

Comments:

_____

_____

_____

_____

_____

_____

_____

_____

_____

ABOUT THE AUTHORS

LaTishia L. Jordan has been a teacher and tutor for a number of years. She started Micheaux's Learning Center in 2005 because she wanted to provide a place for students to receive quality tutorial services that would help students succeed in school and reach their greatest potential.

LaTishia has worked in the field of education for a number of years starting out as a Mathematics tutor for the math department at Bennett College where she received her Bachelor's of Science in Mathematics. LaTishia continued her education at American Intercontinental University where she received a Masters in Information Technology. She continued to work as a private tutor and eventually joined the faculty at Randolph County Community College where she taught in the Business Education department. LaTishia is currently working on a Ph.D. in Education with a specialization in Pre-K through 12 Educational Leadership.

She is a 2008, 2009, and 2010 Nashville Emerging Leader (NELA) award finalist and a member of the Young Leaders Council. LaTishia also owns an additional Learning Center, Nashville Learning Center that she acquired in 2013. She loves to learn and is working on making Nashville Learning Center and Micheaux's Learning Center the best supplemental education providers available to the residents of the Nashville Metropolitan area.

LaTishia is a native of Nashville, Tennessee, where she resides with her Maltipoo, Bentley.

Whitney King obtained her Bachelor's Degree in Sociology at South Carolina State University, a degree in Paralegal Studies from Kaplan University, and a Masters of Arts in Teaching with a concentration in Special Education from Liberty University. Whitney has worked in both public and private school settings in order to gain a better understanding of how to bridge the gap between families and the school. Whitney owns and operates LEAF Learning Center, based in Rockville, MD. LEAF Learning Center caters to youth ages 3-21 with Special Learning Needs, primarily students on the Autism Spectrum. Whitney is a member of Alpha Kappa Psi Professional Business Fraternity, Inc. Whitney is the mother of two beautiful children, McKenleigh & Jordan, and they reside in Maryland.